Balm

DR. KULJIT SINGH JANJUA

BlueRose ONE
Stories Matter
NewDelhi • London

BLUEROSE PUBLISHERS
India | U.K.

For permissions requests or inquiries regarding this publication, please contact:

BLUEROSE PUBLISHERS
www.BlueRoseONE.com
info@bluerosepublishers.com
+91 8882 898 898
+4407342408967

ISBN: 978-93-6783-559-3

Cover Design: Sadhna
Typesetting: Pooja Sharma
Translated By: Prof. Eesha Narang, DAV College, Abohar (Pb)

First Edition: March 2025

Dedicated to My Ancestors
Whose footsteps have guided me
To where I stand today.

Time and space are but physiological colours which the eye makes, but the soul is light

Ralph Waldo Emerson

Preface

This is unpretentious poetry. Plain, direct, honest. The poet isn't straining to prove he is a poet. So he won't go after popular poetic idiom. And you, the reader, won't have to negotiate the customary devices and patterns of the poet's craft.

But it is a difficult and risky choice. Such a poet can be dismissed as a mere verse-maker. But then Kuljit Singh Janjua doesn't versify either. His lines breathe the rhythm – of feel and phrasing, of memory and desire, of thoughtfulness. And all this is expressed in language that is free and economical. This is language shy of extravagance, and it quietly gravitates to crystallisation of experience.

The immigrant's anguish simmers, sometimes boils over. Then an unreal hope, that he will return to his long left home, takes possession of him. The nostalgia may sound uncomplicated, even naive at times, but it is not overdone. So it doesn't wear out either, but glows like a night sky trapped in the memory of a gone day, the illumination enveloping the particles that will neither touch down and settle nor float away.

The nostalgia has just changed guise when the poet tries to hold on to a world from which nature is vanishing and in which love is a receding memory. The romantic yearning (something at once admired and scorned in these hyper-sentimental and cynical times) is a deeper craving for home transferred to memory and displaced onto nature. Its untimely occurrence may appear to be archaising a modern articulation of desire for effect, but it could be read as an intentionally faded, like denims, gesture of defiance, an admission that irony might be the only language to cry in.

And knowing that return is not possible, the poet nests in Punjabi, the language he carried from home when he left home decades ago.

This perhaps explains the plainness and directness of his style. Home is where you can shed all pretences.

Janjua's sensitivity to gender discrimination is timely and touching. He honours women as equals, yet the deep-ingrained patriarchal attitudes sometimes insinuate themselves to manifest as reverse stereotypes. Unresolved questions of history provoke his rage, but it is a restrained rage, often only a gentleman's cultivated frown and sneer. Injustice perturbs him; you feel he has much bottled up inside (maybe it will find a way out in his future work), yet it doesn't enfeeble his will to stay humane.

This is his first book of poems. As such it deserves scrutiny for the signs of his potential. One such sign is his fleeting engagement with the enigma of the self, particularly in relationships. Another is his sense of irony. Still another is a gift for metaphor. His imagination can concretise silence the labourers wrap over their faces. His mind can see corpses lugging their existence over miles and miles.

Potential is promise awaiting redemption. Our early books are the archives of our struggles to find freedom.

I've already begun to wait for the work of which this book is a harbinger.

Rajesh Sharma

Forward

Reading through the first couple of lines of the book, got me see through the poetic-self of Kuljit Singh Janjua. Taking the daughter born to him, in his hands, he says: "I wish/To give so much love to my daughter/To wash off the generations-old/Wounds on daughters; souls/And apply/The balm of respect and regard..." As I went on reading from poem to poem, the essence of his poetry stood out as more and more polished before my eyes. At one place, he writes: The flower blooming in autumn/The waterfall originating in adversities/ The river flowing through the plains/ The trees standing through the storms/ Are all present in his poetry/ He has, definitely, been in love!"

Reading the very next poem 'Memory', you will be very sure that our poet Kuljit also has been in love and that this love of his shows through his own personality and his entire poetic oeuvre. In his poems, there is soulful representation of our times and the mental states we often find ourselves in.

His poems are like clear puffs of wind that leave in our tree-like minds a sensation of freshness. With the feeling of newness, some dry leaves fall and many new come out. Kuljit has named his book, 'Balm.' For the world around, and especially for his hurting home-land Punjab's heart, these poems surely have a balming affect. My heartiest wishes to Kuljit Ji for penning these poems.

Surjit Patar

Dr Kuljit Singh's Poetry Collection 'Balm': The Medicine of Love

Beautiful poetry is like balm that heals the wounds of the soul, by and by. The three types of ailments a man can suffer from are mental ailments, physical ailments and ailments of the soul. Among these three, the worst are the ailments of the soul. This type of poetry dissipates the disease of the soul gradually. The contemporary man is suffering from many ailments. He has to bear with many wounds every moment. Newer events hurt the heart every day. The poem puts balm on the wounded heart and tries to heal it. Aristotle has talked about artistic expression of these non-pertinent, impure, and bad feelings and how they are purified by being released. He has called this process catharsis.

From this perspective, the title of this book, 'Balm', can be read as a metaphor for medicine for the ailments of the soul. The poet intentionally or unintentionally wants to express the purpose of his poetry through this metaphor. The poems in this collection can be read from various perspectives. One, this poetry displaces the fact of the male ego and its classifications; two, it is the cry of the soul of humanity wounded due to the inhuman and irresponsible actions of mankind, and three, there is the search for the relationships of co-existence and love in the age of mechanisation. Perhaps, this is the poetry of human love that applies balm on each tear and cut.

The Punjabi society has been dominated by men and women have always got a marginal place under the pressure of their ego. Having claimed this power in the society, the male pride, places itself at the apex and has established a violent attitude where women, viz., mothers, sisters, wives or daughters have been pushed to the margins. The poems within 'Balm' very lovingly displace these categories established by the male pride. The poet intends to apply the balm of respect on the wounded soul of women with these words:

1.

Now,
I wish
To give so much love to my daughter
To wash off the generations-old
Wounds on daughters' souls
And apply
The balm of respect and regard

2.

Whenever
I feel upset
I share my joys and sorrows
With her

And, sometimes,
We both
Exchange joys and sorrows
These days
Her hand has come to stay
On my head

My male pride,
I have surrendered
At her feet

The creative act of 'surrendering the male pride at the feet of the woman', is clear displacement of the male-centrism predominant since feudal times and the identification of woman's glorious existence and its respectful acceptance. No doubt, this poetry applies balm to the women's souls distressed since centuries.

The balm of love and respect is spread throughout the book. The history of the men of Punjab has been that of split-tear, cracks, cutting and severing. In and around 1947, the villages of Punjab received deep wounds. Dr. Kuljit very patiently pens this history and at the same time applies the balm of affectionate words:

Searching through

My history

I journey

From era to era

From generation to generation

Across years and months

From moment to moment

Crossing

The seven seas,

Five rivers, Bharat and India

I pause at

The land of two and half rivers

Panj-ab

Closing my eyes,

I think of the separated other half

....

I pray that,

Though split into two,

They should always keep flowing

The villages thereof

Should be prosperous,

With their names and places intact

These lines are the speech of love that is the balm for hatred, partition and the communist alliances, for sure. For the personal gains of politicians, religion, caste and language have always been put to stake and Punjab is left to burn in the furnace of hatred. The power-seekers gave speeches of hatred to snatch power and divided people, the divided people massacred both theirs and the other side. It is very necessary to create such words of affection against the hate speeches. The person can still hold on to hope, sympathy and strength out of love even in adverse situations. The poet acknowledges this type of consciousness through the medium of creativity in these words:

The flower

Blooming in autumn

The waterfall

Originating in adversities

The river

Flowing through the plains

The trees

Standing through the storms

Are all present in his poetry

He has,

Definitely,

Been in love!

Jealousy, pride and hatred turn a person's perspective narrow, violent and communal; love and respect connect everyone with the good of all philosophy. This perspective understands the world that exists under the layer of society where the identity and role of the strength of love, within the relationships of societal power, is decided. Here only lies the feel of warmth and greatness of Nature in his poetry. Here only man forgoes his pride before her and herein lies the rise of love and humility.

This is the first book of Dr. Kuljit Singh. Some of the poems don't meet the standards of poetic language, understanding and art but his poetic judgement, determination and natural expression in some other poems will definitely place him in the line of eminent poets. This is my belief. His maiden book of poetry is welcome to the world of poetry.

Atam Singh Randhawa

A Few Words from the Poet's Desk

My family background is connected to Chak Number 129SB, Western Punjab (Pakistan), but I was born in the village of Kukowal, District Hoshiarpur (India). The heart wrenching narratives of partition that I got to hear from the grandparents had such deep impact on my heart that I would be caught in them all the time. In youth, these stories took the shape of poetry and began to expand over the horizon of my mind. I started loving poetry. During the massacre of June, 1984, my poetry took the shape of such pain that the wounds became cancerous and they bleed till date. There is still no 'balm' available that can be applied to these sores for relief.

My initial poems were born out of the pain of this canker. When I had shared these poems with my schoolmates, and college friends, their wet eyes had been the witness to my being a poet. In the company of my friends, I studied Punjabi poetry/ghazal in more depth. The rich poetry of the resourceful poets opened for me the way to the sea of poetry and awakened in me the desire to learn the art of writing poetry. I feel myself to be dwelling along with these poets even today.

Poetry, for me, is food for the soul. In my opinion, poetry is not just the structuring of a few sentences and ideas, rather it is the medicine for all the ailments of the society. Poetry is the alertness to the treatment of all the troubles of our world. Poetry is not just the appeasement of the soul, it is also the clarion call of revolution. The contemporary poem is in revolt against the power centres and this is a good sign for the poet. I have tried to touch upon the multifarious aspects of the universe and upon the pain of the sufferings of entire mankind. I have presented myself before you with a clear heart and day-to-day vocabulary. Your encouragement is eagerly awaited.

Dr. Kuljit Singh Janjua

Contents

1. Balm

Today,
I took
My new-born daughter
In my hands
For the very first time

Her semblance pure
Her face serene, innocent -
On my elated face
Has arisen a cry of pain
Grandmother's and mother's words
Echo in my ears

Their words,
For a daughter
Were only complaints,
"O if
You only had brought us joy,
O if you were born a boy!"

Then, I had been born
And joy had filled them all
The sister's life had been relieved

Now,
I wish
To give so much love to my daughter
To wash off the generations-old
Wounds on daughters' souls
And apply
The balm of respect and regard

***

2. The Primal Point

O creator!
In this new century,
Have you ever stood
At the foundations of ego
And considered?

Is not the primal point of your creativity
The courage, passion and blessings
Of your ancestors?

Hardships sweat
On seeing you,
Achievements
Kiss your feet

O creator!
Never ever let go of
The primal point of your creativity

Seen from this point,
The unforeseen future, too,
Would, surely, look bright

***

3. Nature

The day has broken
The sun is rising
Redness has expanded
In all four directions
Warmth has spread
The sparrow has chirped
The nightingale has cooed
In my ears have echoed, the cuckoo's notes
O Nature!
You are great, you are amazing

***

4. Creativity

I am
Quiet, calm
Complete on the outside
But,
Incomplete inside

Scared of the pitch dark
The void spread within
I closed my eyes

Then suddenly!
Imagination came
Towards me
It held me by the arm
And walked me alongside
I kept walking along

I enjoyed while walking, absorbed while swimming,
Explored while flying -
Jungles, seas and skies
And sinking in the earth,
I have bowed
Before hell

I have circumambulated
The entire earth
I have appeased all gods
I have become complete.

***

5. Daughter

On the day, I got
My first permanent appointment
Abroad
My darling, my lucky charm
Had been born

Hearing her first cry,
I had laughed, cried!
Gazing at her,
I had felt joy
With much affection
I had named her
*'Taqdeer'**

When she walked,
It would feel like
God, himself, had stepped in
I would pay obeisance
To the house, itself

Taqdeer went to hostel
And then,
To her in-laws
Just like to her hostel,
I have returned,
many times,
After paying obeisance
To her matrimonial house
**Taqdeer means Destiny*

***

6. Prurience

I,
Alone,
Had floated
In the time's flow,
Covered long distances
And had reached there
Where everyone had been a stranger

In the deserted garden
Of my heart
Your arrival was
No less than any Puran's

And now,
I get chills
When I find
The Salwans
Roaming around you

***

7. Identity

You,
In memory,
In dreams,
And now,
In my heartbeats
Have come to stay

Your identity
Has expanded within me

Now,
I fail to find
My own self
From within myself

***

8. Treeness

They always
Distributed
And never
Got tired of distributing
Sometimes, the givers of cool breeze
Sometimes, the saviours of earth
The destroyers of heat waves
They always have been
The worshippers of life

They made humans
Crawl, walk
Fed them
And covered their nakedness

And the humans having
Felled them, chopped them, burnt them
Have moved on, towards
Post-modern era

***

9. Yours Lovingly...

Searching through
My history
I journey
From era to era
From generation to generation
Across years and months
From moment to moment

Crossing
The seven seas,
Five rivers, Bharat and India
I pause at
The land of two and half rivers
Panj-ab
Closing my eyes,
I think of the separated other half

Then, the massacre happens again
The uproar resounds
The dream breaks
Returning to myself
I wipe the pain
Spread across my forehead
I pray for the well-being
Of both the Panjabs'
Both sides

I pray that,
Though five be split into two,
They should always keep flowing
The villages thereof
Should be prosperous,
With their names and places intact

In my secret prayer,
The names Toba Tek Singh and
Kukowal
Get pronounced loudly

The segregation of names and places
Has started again, these days
You, too, pray, my dear
That the wish to be together
Should stay alive

Dear Toba Tek Singh
I hope of seeing you soon
Your lovingly
Kukowal

***

10. Father

During partition
Saving his life,
He saved other's lives too
He would check the hunger of daughters and sons
Pressing their stomachs
Put in their mouths,
The roasted grams tied to the end of his turban

Hungry himself,
With the first rays of the sun,
Great-grandfather had reached
The other half
Of the divided earth
He was labelled a refugee
Nonetheless
He remained true to the new kinships
Remembering the Guru's words

Following this panth
Father had become wise
Beyond his years
Touching the soil of the new whereabouts
To his forehead
He had braced himself

Being respectful, always,
Towards the forefathers
Father would replenish this earth
Father would work really hard
He kept becoming one with this earth
And, alongside, he
Kept worshipping letters
Step-by-step,
Practicing the art of letters
He became their devotee

He worshipped this earth
With his hard work,
He built houses,
Explained to everyone
The definition of home,
Taught
The art of humility,
In the hearts of us sons and daughters
He touched the chords of knowledge

On marrying his daughters,
He had been worried
For all the daughters of the village.
Sending me abroad,
His affection for the sons of the village
Had increased much

He had advised me specially
To keep my feet grounded always:
Be respectful towards your livelihood
Distribute whatever the excess is
Now,
I shall take some rest
Then I shall come to visit you
Abroad

I had thought
I shall disclose the news
Of P.R., myself,
On reaching the village

The first news from the village
This morning is:
My father, with such a big heart,
Has passed away
Due to heart attack…

***

11. Woman

Deeper than the sea
Quiet like a still night
The one who weaves dreams
Of varied hues
An epitome of dedication
Never gives up
Never tires
Never fails

Breaking-building
She remains true to her relationships
Listens to everyone's silence, as well
But
Utters not a word of complaint
For she feels hurts, too

The earth is in her feet
Inside her, the firmament
The ocean is in her eyes
Her habit is devotion
In all, a woman 'is' worship

***

12. Maple Leaves

It is autumn season
The maple is undergoing abscission
Its beautiful golden leaves
Have turned lifeless
Have spread like a colourful sheet
To cover the earth

As I walk
The rustle of the leaves
welcomes me
In a wave like pattern
These leaves meet
The source of their origin

They are making a promise
To return again
After autumn

***

13. I Shall Return

Indeed!
Being turned
In the wheel of livelihood,
I have come
A thousand miles away

Mother
Waiting for me,
In dejection,
Don't you tire yourself standing
at the outskirts of our village

I
Shall return soon
And your wait
Will end now

***

14. Linnet

Early morning
The chirping
Of my dear linnet
Is heard in my house

Her utterances
Mixed with the nectareous Air
Produce a heavenly music
Every nook of the house
Becomes sacred
The flowers begin to rejoice,
Being embalmed

Whenever
Dark clouds surface
Above my house
My linnet
wastes no time,
Transforms into an eagle

In her prayers,
Fledgelings, God and home
Are never absent

I pray
For the life of
All the linnets on this earth
So that
All the homes of this earth
Are safe.

***

15. Blessing

Walking in the park,
I have come
To stand by the old tree
From within which my father
Has looked at me

My attention has been drawn
To thirty-three years back
When
Father had chosen for me
The spouse,
A saint by demeanour

But,
He had left untimely
I had turned, then, into a cobblestone

O father!
In this cobblestone,
The being has appeared again
A plumule has sprouted

The wind of desires
Has started blowing again

Come,
Once again,
And place your hand on my head -
Bless me with
Lifelong marital bliss

***

16. Shadow

Do you know?
Whenever
I walk
You also walk
Along with me

I had heard
That shadows don't have faces
But
I am surprised
Within my shadow,
Your face does show up

Do pay attention
To your shadow as well!

***

17. Memory

Whenever
Poetry alights not,
I
Your memories come rushing

Wandering
In your memories,
Soaked in your colour
I, myself,
End up being a poem

***

18. Knots

After a long time
She came again, today
And again, she forgot
To put down from her head
The bundles of misery

With much difficulty
Have I been able to
Unburden her head
But I
Have still not been able
To unfurl the knots within her

And at last!
With more and more pressing
The bundle inside my heart, too,
Has opened up

Now!
Around me
There is nothing
Apart from nothingness

***

19. Love

The flower
Blooming in autumn
The waterfall
Originating in adversities
The river
Flowing through the plains
The trees
Standing through the storms
Are all present in his poetry

He has,
Definitely,
Been in love!

***

20. Memory

When
The red of the sun
Begins to touch
The skin of the earth
When
The dew born out of fog
Is tasted by the flowers and buds
When
The flowing waters
Cleanse as they flow
From this pure place
Arises a fragrance

Believe me!
I miss you so much
At all those times

***

21. Relationship

Whenever
I come across
Some smart, handsome sardar
With a sky-blue turban,
I feel him to be father-like

When
He gives me some advice,
I feel in him the motherly concern

When
Despite his disagreement,
He agrees with what I say
I feel fatherly affection for him

When,
In my sad moments,
He also turns sad
And in my craziness,
He too joins to rejoice
I feel like he's my better-half

Living abroad,
I have come to realise that
Relationships
Are not about just staying together
What is necessary for a relationship
Is the companionship of souls!

***

22. Daisy

Childlike nature
Epitome of care
The fragrance shop
Earned of love
At heart, very clean
You are ever green
O Gerbera Daisy,
Much love to you
And much more love

***

23. The Games of Times

Sometimes,
I desire
That I should
Unfurl all the bundles
Within me
And place them before her, opened

That I should
Unburden the soul
Of the weight it has been carrying

With happiness
I should fill my soul
To the brim
And then,
I get shivers
Thinking
That I, like mad,
Have been participating
The games of times

***

24. Meeting

I,
Leaving behind all worries,
Want to spend each moment
With you

I want to walk,
Step-by-step,
With you

And further,
I want this journey
To just go on

Our destination is
Close by,
Come, let's walk together
But there's
Only one condition
To this union
We shall have to
Pass across
Each other's souls

***

25. Desires

The waves
Make noise in the sea,
Go out of control,
Similarly
When your words, too,
Resound in my ears
The sun of memories
Arises in my heart
Like high tides,
My desires begin to boil
Just then,
I close my eyes
And get to adore you.

***

26. Wish

O sun!
New hope wake up
With your arrival

Life comes to a standstill
When you pause

The existence of night
Finds its confirmation
When you take leave

Light appears
On your arrival,
And darkness is gone

Selfless
Ceaseless practitioner

O sun!
My wish is
To live like you.

***

27. Birds

Flying free of the borders
The beings of the entire earth
The owners of the universe
The prophets of patience

Accepting heat and cold, equally
They go happily as life unfolds
No criticism
No hate
Nor infested with pride
My best friends are birds,
Not the human tribe!

***

28. Your Arrival

Every scene was lifeless
Nature around, colourless
You came
Every single thing
Brimmed with life!

***

29. I Return

Now,
Whenever the village
Shows up in my dreams

I look at the day breaking,
The peasant, farmers walking towards fields
At dawn

The birds coming out of their nests
The workshops
Of the housewives being set up
In the houses

The Bulls, I see,
Shaking the bells around their necks,
Paying obeisance to their livelihood

With the wandering winds,
I myself begin to turn pleasant
Suddenly,
The alarm goes
And I return
To the country of dollars

***

30. Wait

Just like
We had come away from home
Across the seven seas

In the very same fashion,
Our children have crossed
Many seas and moved away from us
The wait for their return
Stays with us always

The son, on the video call,
Gets scolded by the wife,
That he should call oftener
"I have been reduced to half,
Waiting"

The word 'half'
Has hit my ears when I, myself, have grown old
I have remembered
My mother, who, awaiting us,
Had been reduced to half
Had grown old
And awaiting us only,
Returned to the eternal embrace

I,
Have bowed my head,
Before mother's photograph
Hanging on the wall

***

31. Strategy

Open-heartedness on the outside
But small-heartedness within -
This is the dominant,
Very harmful and worldwide trend

It has birthed
Divisions, wars,
Holocausts,
Terrorists

These days,
It has put on
The mask of globalisation
The kings and ministers, all,
Are at its beck and call

I hear
It has labelled the world,
'Global village'
But,
In my own village
'Western Mall'
Has cropped up

***

32. Whirr

If having put the question,
You carve the answer
By yourself
And keep rotating
Like a top
Around your own self
Then,
It is sure
The whirr of misconception
Shall keep increasing

***

33. Distance

From the house outside the village
To the village home, and vice-versa
We would shuttle
We would play and wrestle
For long hours
No one would ever mind

The elder brothers, the young brothers,
Stayed together, under one roof
And common were
Our joys and sorrows

Crying and laughing together
Doing our stuff
Showing resentment and relenting
We were the happy-go-lucky ones

And now,
The distance between the houses
Has grown so much that
It seems unending

Today, once again,
I have tried
To cover that distance,
I have phoned and asked,
"Dear aunt,
Could I, please, visit home?"

***

34. It's Time to Live

We have run enough
Now,
We should stop,
We should measure
The distances we have covered

We have bettered
Our present
It is time to ponder over our past

We should return
To ourselves
Come!
We should live, now

***

35. Home and Abroad

These days
Whenever I sit alone,
I,
Sitting in a foreign land,
Begin to look for my country
Within my own self

Indeed,
This foreign land
Has given me my livelihood,
My prosperity

Yet, I have not
Succeeded
In detaching my roots
From my village

From my memory,
The streets, the meeting areas,
Each and every person
Have never taken leave

I
Am in conversation
With the village, these days!

***

36. She Met Again

Like every other time,
She met again, today
Making promises
Of never leaving again
Like all other times,
She, instantaneously,
Disappeared

From decades,
I have been living
Her promise
Of never leaving again

***

37. Souls

Now
I know
How souls
Get bruised

And how
Souls meet their death
Waiting of someone's arrival
Day after day

I am in love
These days

***

38. Joys and Sorrows

Whenever
I feel upset
I share my joys and sorrows
With her

And, sometimes,
We both
Exchange joys and sorrows

These days
Her hand has come to stay
On my head

My male ego,
I have surrendered
At her feet

***

39. Hondh-Chillar*

These houses without light
You only had wanted
To erase
From the maps

On the dead bodies
Lying in the debris of these houses,
You only had
*Performed tandav***

You, from your side,
Had ensured the erasure
Of our existence

Holding the torch
Of our glorious heritage
We have come to stand
In all preparedness
To fight fresh wars
This time,
It is your turn to face defeat
For sure

**A hamlet in the Rewari district of Haryana destroyed by the communal forces in November 1984.*
***Tandav: The dance of destruction, a profound metaphor in Hindu philosophy for Shiva's role as destroyer.*

***

40. Heaven

Post-marriage,
Happily,
Father had sent me
Abroad
To my destined heaven

I remember his blessings,
"Flourish and prosper"
"Never feel disappointed"

Running around
For this illusory heaven,
Getting tired-exhausted
Shutting my ears
Closing my eyes
Sewing my lips
I have been running since then

Father, look,
I have not been disheartened yet!

***

41. You are I Only

The dream
Of my sleep
The flame
Of my consciousness,
You are the event of
My glee and my flutter

Do visit sometimes,
That I, too, can meet
My own self
From within you

***

42. Existence - Non-Existence

Definitely,
Everyone pays obeisance
To the rising sun
But, at the end,
The sun has to set

Looking at the moon's beauty,
Everyone gets attracted
But
The moon has to disappear too

O my crazy!
What pride over these fleeting breaths?

***

43. It has Learnt How to Die

No one in the city
Feeling terrified
In the event of firing,
These days

The uniform
The rattle of heavy boots
Does not panic its heart

The city has grown used to
Living under the shadows of
Guns and cannons,
Day in and day out

With the horns of the lorries
Blowing,
The consciousness of the city
No longer gets disturbed

Now,
The city never shows any resentment
True that
The city has learnt
How to die!

***

44. Relationships

With ideal,
True, unpolluted,
Deep relations,
We can still
Wish for the golden age

Come, let us,
At least, learn to walk
Holding each other's hands

***

45. Community

Who has ever pierced
The eagle's eye?
Who has ever hunted the lion?
Who has always considered
The earth to be common to all?
Who has turned down
The face of cruelty, every time?

Yes, all this has been accomplished
By the ones who have seen death from close

These are the ones
To have prayed for collective good
They are the ones
To have turned the flow of the rivers

And always remember,
The characteristic of this community
Is like that of the perennial grass

***

46. Coercion

He keeps smiling
In front of people,
Very patient by nature

But!
Today,
His cry has
Pierced the skies

***

47. Gods

Being sold in the squares
Being consumed in the fields
Burning in the heat of the sun
Freezing in extreme cold
Having wrapped their faces with silence
The labourers are roaming
They seem to me like
Innocent penitents
God knows,
For how many more years
Their penance
Is to continue

Their penance is genuine
But they all are unaware
That these days
The gods of this country,
Appeased with strict penance,
Don't bless
They only curse!

***

48. In this Country

O birds!
Be sure of your knowledge
If you wish to fly in this country

In this country
Of hoopoes,
Not only your flight is insecure
But also your feathers are unsafe

***

49. Love

Love
Never fits
Within any categories of business

In the hateful waters
Of this life
Two persons, together, have
The courage to keep afloat
While getting drowned
And, even in drowning,
To keep afloat

Love
Is the determination
To live forever

***

50. Language, Our Existence

We have never
Cared even in the event of overcast skies
Or raining clouds

But now,
Hailstones have been hitting the heart
Of the mother tongue
It is no longer
The time to migrate temporarily
Instead of arranging to stop
These floods

If we look back
At its trajectory,
Our earlier wounds
Have not stopped bleeding
Yet

***

51. Anger 1

I would not have been angered
If the dogs from the burial ground had bitten,
I got angry
When
My own pets
Looked for an opportunity
And bit me

***

52. Anger 2

I would not have been angered
If vultures
Had stolen away the chickens

I am angry
That egrets, in hiding,
Take support from the snakes
To eat men

***

53. Anger 3

I would not have been angered
That Kaido had again taken out enmity*
That the sister-in-law had again placed
Uncooked in place of ready food
I am angry
*That Sahiban***
Instead of going with her brothers,
Has gone to join hands with some gang
And, they, together, have looted
Mirza's house
And have
Murdered him, mercilessly

**Kaido – an antagonist, portrayed as a deceitful and greedy character driven by selfish motives in the tragic love story of Heer Ranjha, one of the iconic folktales of Panjab.*

***Sahiba – is the heroine in the tragic love story Mirza Sahiban, one of the iconic folktales of Panjab.*

Remembering my beloved nephew, Tejeswar Singh Janjua, a budding singer who left us far too soon in his early youth.

***

54. Illusion

The shared spaces
Shared dreams, joys and sorrows
Shared waters
Shared fire for the hearths
Everything got divided

For us,
It was a holocaust
But when the leaders
Celebrate
Calling it independence,
Within me,
Another massacre takes place
And I
Get engaged in
Internal wars

***

55. The Cage aka Corona

There are wings
And there is courage to fly
But
Where is the freedom?

There's a cage
And there's the bird trapped in the cage
Lysol wipes,
Sprays and gloves
On one side

On the other,
Is the antilogy
Piping hot water
Some antibiotics
The tit-bits of home remedies

The fourteen wires
Of this cage
Are breaking
One by one

One day,
The cage will open for sure
The bird will be free
To take flight again

But,
The sky of his share
Has been acquired!

***

56. The Scare of Corona

Knock
Terror
Curfew
Hue and cry
Death after death

Apocalypse in the world
Promotion after promotion
Business and more business
Political pressure,
The foundation of situations
The insult of democracy

Enemy
Always, ready to attack
The powerful ready to evade
The weak

Definitely,
Corona has gone
But
The enemy will attack again

***

57. Corona 2

Corona has gone away
Also the captivity, the fear and the scare
But!
The image of this tragedy
Is not getting erased from the heart

Last night,
Along with the butterfly,
From earth to earth,
From flower to flower,
I tasted the nectar

I am grateful
For the dreams of living
That are safe
Within my heart

***

58. Alone

Knowing
My yearning
My anguish
My dilemma,
She is going away

I am thinking
How horrible
Would the forced company of
A stranger would be

Therefore,
I am teaching me
To be alone

***

59. Water

Journeying
Through the mountains
Flowing towards the ground
Hitting the rocks
Susurrating
It keeps flowing
Pure and serene
Neither stops, nor tires
Like what Nanak called it
'Pani pita' (water, the father)

O father,
My most sincere regards to you

***

60. Carnage

I have heard of
1947, 1965, 1971,
I witnessed 1984 and Godhra

I have been a witness
To the wailing heard from the ruined houses

The burdens of mother and father
Had sent me abroad
But,
In the heart, all of it
Occurs, again and again,
When I watch the bombardment
Happening in Iraq, on the T.V.

***

61. Chak Number 129SB

He has called out in a very loud voice,
"O Basheer!
Wait dear, I'll also join you."

With a strange king of enthusiasm in his eyes,
Father has been roaming
Asking from the Hindu shopkeeper
For something to eat, sharing light conversations
Asking for kites from Baba Hamid

Having ignored
The call of mother
Father has run away
*Saying he's to visit the madrasa**

After being shaken many times
Father has returned
Listless

I asked
Wherefrom came he
He has replied with folded hands
"God's grace, I am saved!
The mob is coming this way
Close all the doors tightly."

I
Am speechless

** School*

***

62. To Live is More Difficult

Without breaths
Without desires
These walking dead
Keep dragging
Their identities
For miles and miles

Inside them,
Black times have stayed

Passing through a life
Worse than dying
What place are they looking for
To live?

***

63. Calamity

The fire of the hearth
The roti on its flame

The saag in the pot*
Butter in the saag
Very tasty
The family used to eat together
Feeling the togetherness

Indeed!
The sun used to burn like fire
We would be at work in the fields
Hungry or satiated

Acres and acres of land
We had already left behind
How we had gathered this one little by little,
Breaking our backs

Such calamity befell
*Lakhs** turned paupers*
Life, itself, then had felt
Like the greatest asset

By the grace of God
We established ourselves again

Then, I, myself, faced dislocation
Have settled in a foreign land
Ofcourse
There are no financial constraints here
But I feel blessed that
The Panjab, within my heart,
Has not been displaced

**Saag – leafy green vegetable*
***Lakhs - hundreds of thousands*

***

64. Barren

You
Made every effort
To turn me barren
But,
The courage, the passion, the dedication
Of my sons
Has not been dismissed

My gentle sons
Having come together
Are safeguarding the land
They have won again
*The power centre, Delhi**

Now, my sons
Would not be careless
O ruler!
Now on, my dear sons
Would not lose to you
I have firm faith

**Delhi – house of The People's Assembly (Lok Sabha), parliament of India*
(Remembering the farmers' revolt in Delhi, India)

***

65. That girl

Eyes like a deer
A soft fairy
Hair like the dark night
Milky-white complexion -
That stranger girl
Who had never
Felt like a stranger to me

We studied together
Moved forward,
Kept moving on
Wished each other well

History repeated itself
The parents approved of
A mismatched-marriage
A foreign land seemed like heaven
And she was trapped therein

Having brought down the home of her wishes
She established a household
She accepted the relationship

Sometimes, over a phone call,
She spells out the pain of the imposed relationship
Sitting miles away from me,
She has said again, today,
"You please don't go away from me, ever"

***

66. I Have Been Rekindled

From
So close
Someone has called to
Me

Air has touched
The flickering me,
I
Have been rekindled

***

67. Autumn Will Come

The famished faces
Of the peasants
Have turned lifeless
Now,
Autumn will come

***

68. Mother Tongue

First,
They asked me
To speak in a low voice

Then, they said
That I should speak
In their language

Then they imposed
The adjectives of their own language
They wished to mould
My speech
To match it with their market's

Last night,
Mother visited me again
In a dream
She,
Cleaning the floor,
Picked up a sheet of newspaper
Touched it with her forehead

I have resigned
Today
From this job

***

69. Partition

Suddenly,
Sometimes, in the middle of the night
My grandmother
Wakes up
And words spill out of her mouth,

"O my God,
The chest containing my nose pins,
The top-sheets with knotted ends,
The pillow cases with floral work,
O my almighty God,
The dowry that I prepared for my daughter
Is turning into trash."

Getting up from the cot
She moves her hands here and there
As if looking for something

And, after such long time
Of having left the other side,
From the palatial house,
She starts looking for
That kutcha house
Wherein lies
The living memory of her youthful days

***

70. Prayer

That all lamps
Of every family
Keep burning -
I have always
Asked for this in my prayers

This light of worship,
Its divine grace
Attracts us also
But what can overcome
The want of food

The oil stolen from
Both kindled and extinguished
Earthen lamps
at the graves of
Your ancestors,
Collected
Drop by drop,
Shall keep our hearths,
Gone cold, burning

You also,
Please pray sometimes
That our hearths should
Have fire in them

***

71. Grasscutters' Sons

Whenever his cobbler father
Said to him,
"Son, the sons of a grasscutter
Will be grasscutters only,"
He would bite the pain
Arisen from his heart
With his teeth
He would run way
He would sit in the cremation ground
With a book
He would read to his fill
There, no one would call him
No one would watch over

Within that boy, Pamma,
Coming to our house as labourer,
My father had seen
His talent,
The fire burning within him -
The flame of words

The worshipper of words
The ceaseless devotee of work
The son of the cobbler, Harnam,
Pamma had returned to the village
Having become a doctor

I still remember
The statement he had made,
"It is not at all necessary
That the son of a grasscutter
Should become a grasscutter,
Generation after generation.

***

72. A Lover of Letters

Wheatish complexion
Very pure at heart
A smiling face always
He would never go to school
Without my company
A lover of words he was,
My dear friend, Husan Lal

But, on reaching school,
When he would look at
The Sanskrit teacher Hariya's face
Husan would begin to be
Just opposite his name
He would walk, hiding behind me
In the class, he would sit
Hiding his face

Master Hari Ram
Would get hold of him at last
For some reason or the other
Would curse him for his caste
He would beat Husan so much
That everyone's soul would tremble

Husan's determination
To never withdraw
His relationship with words
Paid off
He was the first one in his generation
To get a government job

Husan remains happy now
With his reputation, in the changed world,
But even today
His complexion begins to change
To blackish hues
When the Hariya master,
Sitting in the minds of his favourite people
Looks at him with squint-eyes

***

73. Grace

When I found you
All darkness was taken away,
In place of deadliness spread around
Every rotting heart
Had been cooled

There is only one God
And his existence is resolute

You blessed us with grace
We broke down
The deadly fence of culture

You taught us the lesson
Of great service
You showed us the path of donation
You made mandatory the law
Of co-operation
You taught us the art
Of fearless living

But!
Once our appetites were appeased
Century after century
We have gone so far
That one-tenth of our earnings
We haven't sent
To your loved poor ones

O Baba ji!
Grant us the grace
To return to you
So that
Walking on this road of determination
We too shall grow and expand
In all four directions...

***

74. Haiku

Pitch dark,
I witnessed the twinkling beetles
While returning from work

Open sky
The temple rising
In the midst of the workers' huts

The noise of strong current
The outsider admires
The birds flying towards their nests

The fragrant wind blew
Her picture, hanging in my heart,
Smiled

The winding creeper
Is rejoicing with the branches
In the splendour of spring

The setting sun
Kept its pace
The quiet spread around, turned scarlet

Peak noon
Waiting for the letter
The newly-wed stands at the door

Drenching rainstorms
The beaten tree
Sticks falling from the nests

The set sun
The bird sitting on the deserted tree
Looking here and there

The month of January
Bright sunshine
The mother makes dung cakes

At dusk time
The birds flying in the sky,
Still far away from home

***

Appendix

I was born in a small village, Kukowal in Distt. Hoshiarpur (India). In the unexpected event of the partition, my family had been uprooted from Chak Number 129SB, Western Punjab (Pakistan) and we came to live in Eastern Punjab (India). In my childhood, I lived with my grandparents and the narratives I heard from them regarding the partition of 1947 have come to stay with me forever. When I grew up, I witnessed the wars of 1965 and 1971. As I stepped into youth, the tragedy of 1984 happened. A few families of my own village were victims of this tragedy. All these events had a deep impact on me and my creative process.

I began writing poetry when I was doing my matriculation at Doaba Sikh National High School, Nawanshahr Doaba, District Jalandhar. My classmate Paramjit Chumber loved to write poems and songs. I too began to try rhyme taking inspiration from him. I would write something and reading it to my friends Paramjit Chumber, Varinder Gill, Jaswinder Dayal, Sukhvir Kandola and Lally Atwal, I would get applause from them. The appreciation by my friends not only raised my self-confidence, but also inspired me for reading literature. In literature, especially in poetry, I would find much joy and my heart would be transported to some other land. By and by, I read the poetry, ghazals, and songs of Prof. Mohan Singh, Bawa Balwant, Shiv Kumar Batalvi, Amrita Pritam, Dr. Jagtar, Randhir Singh Chand, Surjit Patar, Ajaib Kamal, Sant Ram Udaasi and Lal Singh Dil. All these poets had much influence on me and I have been reading them since college days. Poetry, for me, is the food for soul and I love to dwell in the world of poesy. To keep this passion alive, I have also set up a small library in my house itself.

I migrated to Montreal (Canada) in September, 1992. I wrote my first poem in Canada on the 25th of September, addressing my mother.

It gets difficult to find jobs in Montreal in the winter months and I, too, was jobless for a while. I had all the time to read and learn. I came into the fold of poetry once again. In those days, a weekly newspaper named 'Punjabi Duniya' used to be published from Toronto. I started sending my poems to them and the editor of the newspaper, Tarsem Singh 'Panchi' began publishing them. After a few months, I got busy in work and my interest in poetry declined. I could hardly write a word.

In 2001, one day, during lunch time, I found an employee in my office, named Manjinder, reading the book 'Mein Udan Vich Haan' by a Punjabi poet Dalvir Singh Aasi. On asking, she told me that she has done MA in Panjabi and she has much interest in poetry. She had brought many books along with her from Punjab; I borrowed some books from her and started reading them. My relationship with literature was re-established.

In 2007, I came in touch with my childhood friend Paramjit, who lives in America these days. We started exchanging our poems on Facebook. In the year 2009, with the efforts of Prof. Darshan Singh Bains and Sardar Piara Singh Kudowal, I got associated with the literary group 'Kalm Language Foundation of North America'. I actively participated in the Punjabi Conferences organized by this forum and in the years 2013-14, I was also chosen as its President. These were the days when I came in touch with many eminent poets and writers, and got to learn the nuances of writing poetry. This trend has continued till date. The writers Janab Munir Niazi, Janab Sharif Kunjahi, Afzal Sahir, Baba Najmi, Prof. Ashiq Raheel, Prof. Tariq Gujjar and Saleem Pasha are my favourite writers from Western Panjab and I read them often. Prof. Ashiq Raheel and Saleem Pasha reside in the Toronto region now, and sometimes, I get to talk with them regarding poetry at literary gatherings.

In my opinion, poetry is not just words but it is about decoding the turbulences of a poet's mind, meditating on them and thought process of sorting things out. The main themes of my poems are nature, universe, love, partition of 1947, fields, violence and the atrocities of the powerful tyrants, workers, peasants, women's (mothers, sisters, daughters) emotions.

The structure and the language of the poem should be such that the common reader could follow it; this too, I believe, is an achievement of a poem. I have tried to be true to this statement as far as possible in these poems.

In the past few years, I was asked by many literary friends to publish my work but I had been reluctant. At last, this present book, 'Balm' has been published in 2025 and is presented in the court of the readers. I hope they would like my poems and encourage me to write further!

Special Thanks

I am thankful to my school friends and the first readers, and listeners of my poems viz., Dr. Paramjit Chumber, Dr. Varinder Gill, Jaswinder Dayal, Sukhvir Kandola, and Lally Atwal, who appreciated me and boosted my self-confidence.

I am grateful to the entire team of 'Naksh' (quarterly Punjabi Magazine) and especially its editor Ms. Sonia Manjinder, who kept me engaged with literature and encouraged me to publish this book.

I thank Dr. Rajesh Sharma ji, who not only wrote the preface of the book but also gave valuable advice and constructive feedback from time to time.

I am indebted to my friends Prof. Tariq Gujjar, Afzal Sahir, Saleem Pasha, IjAj Ali, Ahmed Raza Watoo and Anjum Gill from the Western Panjab (Pakistan) who inspired me to publish the book.

I sincerely thank Prof. Eesha Narang of DAV College, Abohar (Punjab), for her outstanding effort in translating my poems into English.

I owe my gratitude to Surjit Patar ji who read my book and introduced me to the readers with his valuable words.

Last but not least, I extend my gratitude to the entire team at BlueRose Publications for helping me bring out my first book of poems in English, Balm.